EXPLORING COUNTRIES

The Czech Republic

by Walter Simmons

BELLWETHER MEDIA · MINNEAPOLIS, MN

Note to Librarians, Teachers, and Parents:

Blastoff! Readers are carefully developed by literacy experts and combine standards-based content with developmentally appropriate text.

Level 1 provides the most support through repetition of high-frequency words, light text, predictable sentence patterns, and strong visual support.

Level 2 offers early readers a bit more challenge through varied simple sentences, increased text load, and less repetition of high-frequency words.

Level 3 advances early-fluent readers toward fluency through increased text and concept load, less reliance on visuals, longer sentences, and more literary language.

Level 4 builds reading stamina by providing more text per page, increased use of punctuation, greater variation in sentence patterns, and increasingly challenging vocabulary.

Level 5 encourages children to move from "learning to read" to "reading to learn" by providing even more text, varied writing styles, and less familiar topics.

Whichever book is right for your reader, Blastoff! Readers are the perfect books to build confidence and encourage a love of reading that will last a lifetime!

This edition first published in 2012 by Bellwether Media, Inc.

No part of this publication may be reproduced in whole or in part without written permission of the publisher. For information regarding permission, write to Bellwether Media, Inc., Attention: Permissions Department, 5357 Penn Avenue South, Minneapolis, MN 55419.

Library of Congress Cataloging-in-Publication Data
Simmons, Walter (Walter G.)
 The Czech Republic / by Walter Simmons.
   p. cm. – (Blastoff! readers) (Exploring countries)
 Includes bibliographical references and index.
 Summary: "Developed by literacy experts for students in grades three through seven, this book introduces young readers to the geography and culture of the Czech Republic"–Provided by publisher.
 ISBN 978-1-60014-728-9 (hardcover : alk. paper)
 1. Czech Republic–Juvenile literature. I. Title.
 DB2065.S55 2012
 943.71–dc23   2011029473

Printed in the United States of America, North Mankato, MN.

010112   1203

Contents

Germany

Poland

★ Prague

Czech Republic

Austria

N
W E
S

Did you know?
The Czech Republic formed in 1993. This is when Czechoslovakia split into Slovakia and the Czech Republic.

Slovakia

The Czech Republic is a **landlocked** country in central Europe that covers 30,451 square miles (78,867 square kilometers). Neighboring countries include Germany to the west and Austria to the south. Slovakia lies across the southeastern border, and Poland lies to the northeast.

The Czech Republic consists of three regions. Bohemia takes up the western half of the country. In the east, Moravia covers the rest of the land except for the small region of Silesia on the border with Poland. Prague lies on the banks of the Vltava River in Bohemia. It is the capital and largest city of the Czech Republic.

The Bohemian **Plateau** covers most of the Czech Republic. It is surrounded by a series of mountain ranges and valleys. Dense forests of pine and spruce trees cover the steep hills of the Šumava Mountains in the southwest. The highest point in the Czech Republic is Sněžka, at 5,256 feet (1,602 meters) tall. This mountain is part of the Krkonoše, or Giant Mountains.

The Elbe River begins near Sněžka and flows into Germany. The Jizera, Vltava, and Ohre are **tributaries** that join this river in the Czech Republic. The Odra River begins as a small mountain stream near the town of Ostrava. From there, it runs north into Poland and empties into the Baltic Sea.

Sněžka

Did you know?

The Moravian Karst is a region of rocky cliffs and limestone towers in the eastern part of the Czech Republic. Explorers have found more than 1,000 caves near the surface, many with underground rivers.

The Vltava River

The Vltava River is the longest river in the Czech Republic. It provides a useful waterway for people and goods. This river has its **source** in the Bohemian Forest. It flows for 270 miles (435 kilometers) and then meets the Elbe River.

Along the way, large dams block the river. The dams create **reservoirs**, where people enjoy boating and swimming. The rushing water turns massive **turbines** in the dams. The turbines generate much of the electricity in the Czech Republic.

grebe

little owl

mouflon

The landscape of the Czech Republic is home to many different animals. Deer and wild boars live in highland forests. The **endangered** mouflon climbs high in the mountains. Small wolf packs prowl along the border of Slovakia. Lynx and black bears hunt in the forests of the Šumava Mountains, where wild rabbits and minks must always be on guard.

Loons, grebes, and pelicans are just a few of the many birds in the Czech Republic. Eagles, kites, and falcons search for prey in the forests and mountains. Hunters track geese, ducks, pheasants, and other **game birds**. The country is also home to 11 different owl **species**.

11

The People

More than 10 million people live in the Czech Republic. Nine out of every ten have Czech **ancestors**. Others have ancestors from Slovakia, Poland, Germany, and Hungary. Roma also live in the Czech Republic. These people arrived in Europe from India centuries ago.

Czech is the official language of the Czech Republic. Some people also speak Slovak. Polish speakers are common in the north, and many people on the western border speak German. **Immigrants** speak other languages, including Russian, Albanian, and Ukrainian.

Speak Czech!

English	Czech	How to say it
hello	ahoj	uh-HOY
good-bye	nashledanou	NOSK-le-DON-oh
yes	ano	AH-no
no	ne	neh
please	prosím	PRO-seem
thank you	dékuji	DECK-kwee
friend (male)	kamarád	KAH-mah-rod
friend (female)	kamarádka	KAH-mah-rod-kah

In cities, many Czech families live in apartments. The old streets in the center of town are narrow, and most people ride bikes or walk to get around. The **suburbs** have more space. Houses have lawns and sidewalks, and some have a garage for the family car. People shop at small shops, grocery stores, and street markets. New shopping malls offer a variety of goods from all over the world.

Life in the countryside moves more slowly. People live in houses on farms or near smaller villages. People in the countryside must travel farther to shop than those in the city. They use cars, buses, and trains to get to bigger cities.

Where People Live in the Czech Republic

countryside 26%

cities 74%

Many Czech kids begin their education in kindergarten, which can last up to three years. Then they must attend five years of primary school. Secondary school follows, and students attend for four years.

Some students then choose to study at **gymnasium**. There they can focus on a single area of study. Students talented in the arts often attend **conservatories**. After secondary school, some students go to a **vocational school**. This is where they learn skills for specific jobs. Other students continue their education at a university.

Did you know?
The Czech Republic is famous for its glass, which is sold around the world.

Where People Work in the Czech Republic

manufacturing 39%

farming 3%

services 58%

Most Czech workers have jobs in services or manufacturing. Czechs with **service jobs** work in banks, stores, hotels, and other places that serve people. Czech factory workers make clothing, electronics, shoes, and appliances.

The Czech Republic has large areas of **fertile** soil and land rich in **minerals**. Farmers raise livestock and grow sugar beets, potatoes, and grains. Miners dig coal, **uranium**, tin, and other minerals from the ground. One of the most important minerals is kaolin. This soft white rock goes into paper, paint, dishes, and even toothpaste!

The Czech Republic has sent many professional hockey players to the National Hockey League in the United States. Jaromír Jágr was one of the youngest players to score a goal in the Stanley Cup finals.

Ice hockey and soccer are the most popular team sports in the Czech Republic. Athletes join local clubs if they want to play these sports. The mountains of the Czech Republic attract hikers and climbers. In winter, skiers and snowboarders hit the slopes while others cross-country ski. Windsurfing and canoeing are popular on lakes and reservoirs.

Czechs also enjoy music, dancing, and other activities. Many in the cities attend concerts and plays. People often play chess, **backgammon**, and other board games at sidewalk cafés.

fun fact

In the Czech Republic, no dish is complete without tangy sauerkraut, made from red or white cabbage.

The Czech Republic is famous for its **hearty** food. **Dumplings** are a Czech specialty. *Knedlíky* are small bread dumplings that Czechs eat any time of day. Cooks prepare them with pastry dough and fillings such as meat, vegetables, or fruit. *Palacinky* are rolled-up pancakes with fruit or chocolate inside. Families in both the city and countryside enjoy wild game, including roast boar, hare, and venison.

Czechs often enjoy a small breakfast of bread with coffee or tea. Lunch is the big meal of the day. Many people go home at midday to enjoy soup, potatoes, and a meat dish. Evening meals are small, sometimes just soup and bread with cheese. A favorite soup is Hunter's Mushroom Soup. It is made with mushrooms, onions, bacon, and cream.

Hunter's Mushroom Soup

knedlíky

palacinky

The Czech Republic celebrates several national and religious holidays. Czechoslovak Founding Day falls on October 28. On this day in 1918, the Czechs and Slovaks won independence from the Austro-Hungarian Empire. On January 1, the country celebrates the founding of the Czech Republic in 1993.

Most Czechs celebrate Christmas and Easter. At Christmas, families get together and have traditional meals of fresh carp and roast turkey. Czechs have named most days of the year after an important Christian **saint**. If a person shares their name with the saint of the day, it is their *svátek*, or name day. Others offer good wishes and may give a small gift!

Prague's nickname is "The City of 100 **Spires**." Tall towers rise from castles and churches throughout the capital city. In the middle of the city, the famous Charles Bridge crosses the Vltava River. Skilled **masons** finished the bridge in the early 1400s.

Near the bridge is the famous Dancing House. This strange building looks like a pair of dancers. Nearby, people stroll along the **cobblestone** streets of *Staré Město*, the "old town." Prague Castle looks over the city from a hill. This castle is the largest in the world. It has become a symbol of the Czech people's pride in their history, culture, and independence.

Dancing House

Prague Castle

fun fact

The name Prague comes from the word *praga*, which means "ford." In ancient times, an important river crossing, or ford, was located here.

Fast Facts About the Czech Republic

The Czech Republic's Flag

The flag of the Czech Republic has horizontal bands of white and red, and a blue triangle. The three colors are the traditional colors of Bohemia. The flag was adopted in 1920.

Official Name: Czech Republic

Area: 30,451 square miles (78,867 square kilometers); the Czech Republic is the 116th largest country in the world.

Capital City:	Prague
Important Cities:	Brno, Ostrava, Plzeň, Olomouc
Population:	10,190,213 (July 2011)
Official Language:	Czech
National Holiday:	Czechoslovak Founding Day (October 28)
Religions:	None (59%), Christian (29%), Other (12%)
Major Industries:	construction, farming, manufacturing, mining, services
Natural Resources:	coal, clay, graphite, kaolin, timber, tin, uranium
Manufactured Products:	cars, machinery, electronics, clothing, shoes, paper products, chemicals, glass products
Farm Products:	wheat, rye, oats, corn, barley, hops, potatoes, sugar beets, poultry, hogs, cattle
Unit of Money:	Czech koruna; the koruna is divided into 100 haleru.

Glossary

ancestors—relatives who lived long ago

backgammon—a game of skill and chance played with a board, pieces known as checkers, and dice

cobblestone—a large, flat stone; many older streets in Europe are paved with cobblestones.

conservatories—schools that train students in the fine arts, such as music, theater, and dance

dumplings—balls of dough often filled with meat or vegetables

endangered—at risk of becoming extinct

fertile—supports growth

game birds—birds that are hunted for sport and for food

gymnasium—a secondary school option where students can focus on a specific area of study

hearty—filling and comforting

immigrants—people who leave one country to live in another country

landlocked—completely surrounded by land

masons—skilled workers who cut and fit building stone together

minerals—elements found in nature; kaolin, tin, and uranium are examples of minerals.

plateau—an area of flat, raised land

reservoirs—large lakes formed by river dams

saint—a person honored by the Christian faith

service jobs—jobs that perform tasks for people or businesses

source—the place where a stream or river begins to flow

species—specific kinds of living things; members of a species share the same characteristics.

spires—towers that come to a point on top of buildings

suburbs—communities that lie just outside a city

tributaries—streams or rivers that flow into larger streams or rivers

turbines—engines that generate electricity from wind or water power

uranium—a metal that serves as fuel for nuclear reactors

vocational school—a school that trains students to do specific jobs

To Learn More

AT THE LIBRARY
Press, Petra. *Czech Republic*. San Diego, Calif.:
Lucent Books, 2002.

Sioras, Efstathia, and Michael Spilling. *Czech Republic*. New York, N.Y.: Marshall Cavendish Benchmark, 2010.

Taus-Bolstad, Stacy. *Czech Republic in Pictures.*
Minneapolis, Minn.: Lerner Publications Co., 2003.

ON THE WEB
Learning more about
the Czech Republic
is as easy as 1, 2, 3.

1. Go to www.factsurfer.com.

2. Enter "The Czech Republic" into the search box.

3. Click the "Surf" button and you will see a list of related Web sites.

With factsurfer.com, finding more information is just a click away.

Index